DESIGN DIARY

NOEL JEFFREY

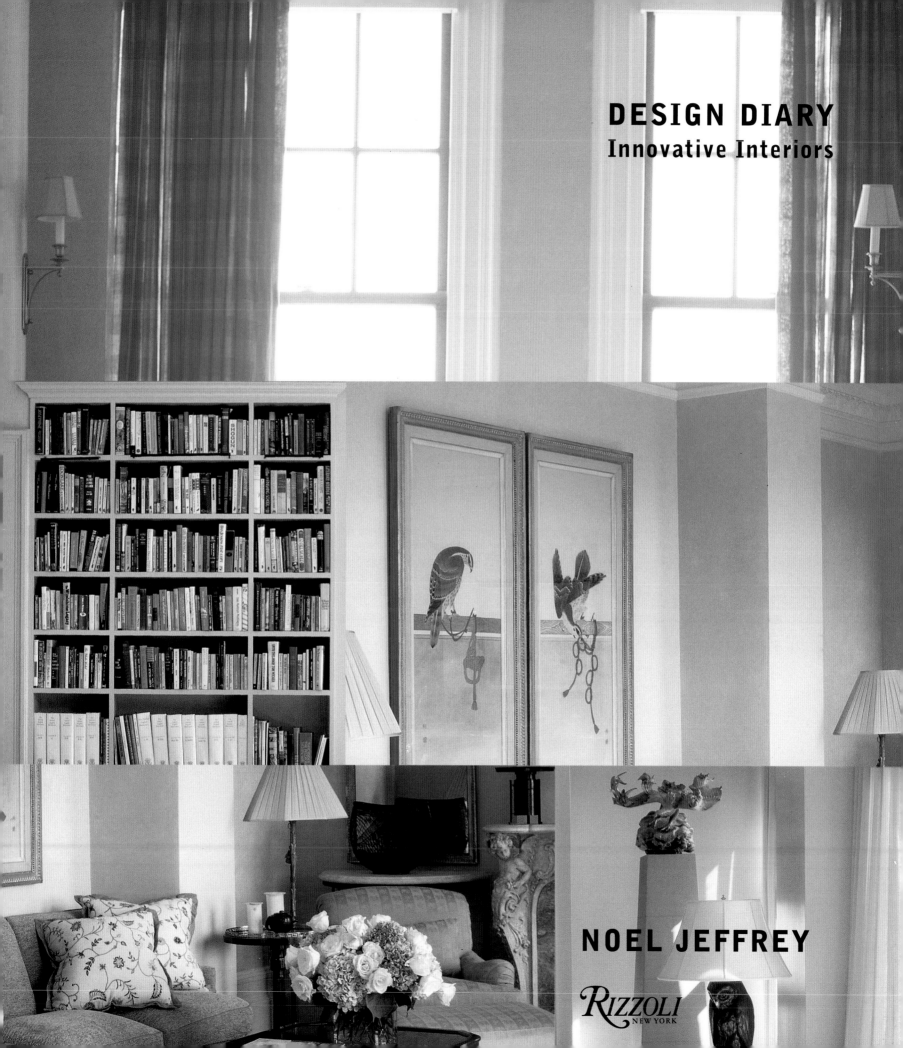

DESIGN DIARY
Innovative Interiors

NOEL JEFFREY

RIZZOLI
NEW YORK

First published in the United States of America in 2001 by
RIZZOLI INTERNATIONAL PUBLICATIONS, INC.
300 Park Avenue South
New York, NY 10010

ISBN: 0-8478-2408-X
Library of Congress Control Number: 2001087574

Distributed by St. Martin's Press

Printed and bound in China.

For Mother and Dad

CONTENTS

INTRODUCTION

For more than thirty years, I have been an active member of the interior design community in New York City. It has been an extremely rewarding and exciting endeavor. The people I have met, the things I have learned, and the creative challenges I have faced have greatly enriched my life.

Many clients have asked me to explain to them the secrets of the trade and the "insider" information on how interior designers can take a space, mix in various materials, furniture, accessories, artwork, and other ingredients, and end up with a real home and not just another "decorated" interior. So, after much thought and some reflection I present to you *Design Diary: Innovative Interiors*, a compendium of my own design experiences, reflections, ideas, and observations on this fascinating and exciting field.

This book is intended to be used as an inspirational and informational guide to help you create the home of your dreams, or to provide you with ideas and knowledge as you work with your own interior designer. Each chapter is filled with large, full-color photographs and detailed close-ups, as well as floor and furniture plans when they were available. In addition, a list of designer's tips in each chapter provides specific information about how to create sumptuous interiors in your own home.

Your home is your refuge. Use this book to inspire and inform you on how to design your own space. Remember, there are no design problems, only design challenges, and each one provides an opportunity to discover and to explore new ways to fashion the perfect home. I hope you enjoy reading and using this book as much as I have enjoyed writing and compiling it. Happy designing!

Noel Jeffrey

A STUDY IN SERENITY

As an interior designer I face many challenges while designing a home for a client. These challenges are what inspire me to create my best work and discover creative and innovative solutions to provide for each client the perfect space they can proudly call home.

I designed this 5000-square-foot apartment for a husband and wife as their refuge. They wanted their prewar duplex, overlooking Central Park, to be a comfortable and stylish haven for their personal enjoyment. They entertained occasionally, but the primary focus of the design had to be for their comfort and enjoyment. Created from two apartments, the duplex required practically all new furniture, accessories, window treatments, rugs, lamps, and so on. The few pieces that were kept were used in guest bedrooms and occasionally in one of the main rooms. For inspiration I turned toward the breathtaking views of Central Park and used a natural theme in subtle ways. Additionally, the clients are avid bird lovers and their collection of bird-related art figured into the apartment's decor.

To fulfill my clients' desire for a restrained, almost countrylike atmosphere in an apartment building located in New York City, I opted for a tranquil color scheme of stone, pale celadon, and a warm, creamy shade of white. This combination provided a common thread among the varied and eclectic pieces used throughout the home.

In the living room, the elaborate crown molding and other architectural details were painted a warm shade of white to highlight them, without having them overwhelm the space. On the walls, a warmer and deeper tone was created with a technique called encaustic. This made the grand space appear more intimate. Encaustic—meant to simulate "Stucco Veneziano"—is a mix of marble dust, gypsum powder, and other textured materials and pigments in a polymer base. Following the trowel applications, the walls were then burnished to a dappled satin sheen with steel blades. The rug, an Indian Amritsar circa 1900, grounds the main conversation area in a colorway of silver, ivory, and taupe. In a neutral palette of light celadon and stone, the fabrics used on the upholstered pieces rely on subtle pattern and tactile texture for visual impact.

To further impart a casual yet elegant air, unlined cotton check curtains—attached to rings and hung on simple rods—soften the edges of the space but do not encumber the overall appearance of the room. Custom-designed hardware with a leaf motif is a subtle gesture to the expansive view of Central Park just beyond the windows. Warm wood tones of mahogany and walnut enhance the comfortable yet sophisticated atmosphere. The coffee table (which I designed) boasts a playful star motif in each corner, picking up the warm golden tones of the sconces attached to the columns, as well as the flower medallions adorning the splats of the chairs encircling the antique George III Manx table. This unusual

(continued on page 17)

Selected antiques, such as the Restauration carved mahogany fauteuil with dolphin-motif arms, in combination with custom-designed pieces and carefully edited artwork and accessories, imbue this living room with a sense of tranquillity and comfort. Columns define various areas within the large room without breaking up the space. Bird-related art and subtle natural decorations such as the custom-designed leaf hardware and subdued floral patterns echo the beautiful window views of Central Park. The subtle yet distinctive color combination of light celadon, stone, and ivory, along with the clean lines and elegant proportions of the furnishings, lend the space an atmosphere of comfort and elegance.

table is raised on a tripod base and boasts carved gentlemen's legs, complete with boots! The antique silver-plated Polish samovar, silver column table lamp, and antique mirror used in the four-part folding screen (which I designed after an early nineteenth-century French original I had admired) add a glittering touch to the serene room. Restrained yet well-selected accessories and artwork further enhance the mood.

A contemporary Japanese basket crafted by Minoura Chikuho and purchased from a gallery in Santa Fe, New Mexico, sits on a console table created from old metal pieces and topped with a piece of limestone. A *Directoire* mirror, circa 1790 in a gilt frame, sits behind the basket. A pair of late nineteenth-century Japanese watercolors of hawks, purchased from a prominent London art gallery, is symmetrically hung behind the sofa.

The dining room continues the elegantly restrained atmosphere. Bare wood floors, stained a warm tone of walnut, are laid in a herringbone pattern to add interest and subtle detail to the room. A large English Regency–style dining table is encircled by six of the twelve armchairs found in the dining room. These Empire mahogany chairs are signed by the famous furniture maker Jacob and date from 1810. A 1940s-era Venetian glass chandelier seems to float above the center of the table, where a monumental, acid-etched centerpiece bowl signed Daum from the 1920s resides.

WHEN SELECTING ACCESSORIES FOR YOUR
HOME, REMEMBER TO BUY WHAT YOU LOVE
AND DISPLAY ITEMS SO THAT NOTHING
DETRACTS FROM THEIR GRACE AND
BEAUTY. A SINGLE OBJECT SUCH AS THE
BEAUTIFUL CONTEMPORARY BASKET
SHOWCASED ON A CONSOLE TABLE IN THIS
HOME, IS DISPLAYED TO ITS BEST
ADVANTAGE WHEN OTHER OBJECTS (WHAT I
CALL VISUAL NOISE) ARE EDITED OUT OF A
TABLETOP VIGNETTE. AS THE FAMOUS
ARCHITECT MIES VAN DER ROHE STATED,
"LESS IS MORE."

From the quilted silk upholstery on the suite of antique Empire
dining chairs to the painted block finish on the walls, this dining
room is a subtle contrast of graphic patterns. The herringbone floor
plays nicely off the subtle stripe in the drapes, the reeding on the
George III console, and the harlequin top of the 1940s French
breakfast table. Subtle tones of light celadon, stone, and ivory
continued from the living room impart a sophisticated yet simple
aura in the room.

 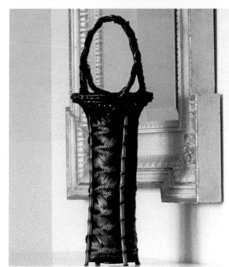

As in the rest of the home, the kitchen is a serene, comfortable mix of subtle pattern, color, texture, and materials. The stainless steel countertops in combination with the custom cooktop hood and glass-fronted cabinets add shimmer and sparkle to this room. Stenciled in a harlequin pattern, the floor repeats the graphic pattern introduced in the nearby dining room.

For a more intimate dinner or a cozy spot for a breakfast for two, a 1940s light oak French breakfast table is placed directly in front of the window. The inlaid harlequin pattern on the top of the table provides a subtle graphic counterpoint to the pattern of the wood floor. Striped floor-to-ceiling silk draperies further enhance this graphic juxtaposition, while softening the hard planes of the room.

As in the living room, accessories and artwork are subdued yet rich in impact and statement. A pair of bronze late nineteenth-century Meiji–period candlesticks flank either end of the fireplace mantle. A Japanese basket crafted to look like bamboo sits atop one of a pair of George III giltwood demilune consoles with a white carrara marble top. One of a pair of turn-of-the-century Belle Epoque–style painted and parcel gilt mirrors sits right above. The result is a dining room perfectly suited for a large dinner party or an intimate meal for two.

This kitchen (there are two in the apartment) continues the comfortable yet sophisticated palette established throughout the rest of the home. A stenciled harlequin pattern on the wood floor is reminiscent of the breakfast table in the nearby dining room. Stainless steel countertops provide a surface for food preparation and other tasks that is both practical and aesthetic. The attractive stainless steel and brass stove hood hangs directly above the cooking peninsula to provide a handy spot for cookware and utensil display and storage.

Antiques and upholstered pieces beautifully coexist in this stately, cozy room. Subdued fabrics, warm-toned wood pieces in mahogany, and beautiful artwork and accessories create an inviting private space. The bird-related artwork, contemporary English owl lamp, leaf-inspired drapery hardware, and subtle botanical-patterned carpet remind us that Central Park is just outside the windows.

Upper cabinets boast glass doors that exhibit favorite kitchenware and add sparkle to the room. Schoolhouse pendant light fixtures provide ample ambient and task lighting and continue the relaxed, countrylike atmosphere the clients desired.

The library was designed to provide a spot to read, to handle correspondence, or simply to sit and watch television. We redesigned the existing bookcases to house the clients' impressive personal library, as well as to display favorite pieces of artwork. A subtle leaf-patterned broadloom area rug continues the nature theme introduced throughout the rest of the home.

Mahogany antique occasional tables provide warm accents in this serene space. A large William IV partners' writing table flanked by a pair of contemporary gray leather-upholstered chairs provides a perfect place to sit and answer letters or play chess. Simple sheer wool casement curtains are hung from custom hardware and puddle slightly on the floor, adding a note of softness to the room.

As in the rest of the home, the master bedroom is a study in serenity and comfort. I designed the four-poster bed out of iron to make a strong design statement without overwhelming the space. French polished mahogany rings hold sheer wool casement bed curtains edged in a hand-woven design by the prominent New England weaver Sam

(continued on page 29)

Kasten. The crewel coverlet in a soothing combination of ivory and sand is fabricated from an English material; it continues the natural theme with its overall pattern of intertwined flowers, leaves, and vines. A similar pattern is reintroduced in the rug, anchoring the bed area of the room. A pair of mahogany side tables and a Japanned tray table (already in the clients' furniture collection) add a punch of color to the tranquil setting without affecting the overall mood. A banquette placed directly in front of the window provides a contemplative place to read or daydream. Uncomplicated Roman shades, crafted from cream-colored silk and blackout lined, provide a touch of softness for my clients' private refuge, as well as a means to control the ample natural light from the windows.

Designing a beautiful home with entertaining as a focus is a delightful challenge. But designing a beautiful space with comfort and refuge as the primary focus is an even greater one—one that I think has been successfully realized here.

As in the rest of the home, the master bedroom is designed in striking but subtle contrasts. Neutral fabrics, interesting textures, and varying materials create a restful refuge in this prewar apartment. Wall mounted swing-arm sconces provide task lighting for nighttime reading and keep bedside tabletops free from clutter and visual noise.

SECOND TIME AROUND: FOR THE LOVE OF ART

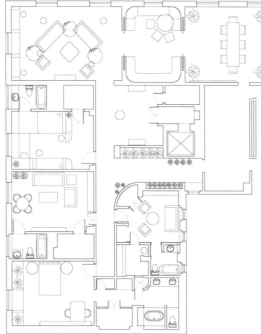

1978 design

DESIGN TIP

SOFTEN ANGULAR, SHARP-EDGED

SPACES BY CHOOSING FURNITURE

WITH CURVED EDGES AND ROUNDED

FORMS TO COUNTERACT THE SHARP

PLANES AND ANGLES.

One of the greatest rewards interior designers reap from working with clients is the satisfaction of knowing that they were able to accurately interpret the needs and wants of the client and meld that with their own experience, knowledge, education, and aesthetic sense. When a client looks around the home and states, "It's exactly what I wanted," you know, as a designer, that you have succeeded to the highest level in utilizing your expertise, training, and taste.

For more than thirty years, I've designed my clients' homes with them in mind. After I've finished with a design, I leave and go on to new projects. The clients live with the designs I have created especially for them. The greatest satisfaction I can receive as a designer is when, after a period of time, a client contacts me requiring my design services to decorate a new home, design a second or vacation home, or update a space I previously created.

One of my favorite projects was a 4000-square-foot prewar apartment located in Manhattan that I completed in 1978. The apartment is home to a couple who are avid art collectors as well as philanthropists. The design challenge was to create a home that would showcase their important art collection, as well as provide a comfortable and beautiful space that would allow them to entertain frequently for their various philanthropic activities. This was achieved through the use of custom-designed and carefully selected

(continued on page 33)

30

furniture that highlighted the impressive twentieth-century art collection. The windows were left devoid of any treatment to accent the breathtaking views of the cityscape from every room. Neutral-toned fabrics in subtle shades with heightened textures added interest and detail without detracting from the art and accessories. The highly reflective surfaces of glass tabletops, metal bases, and polished wood further enhance the lighting in each room and provide a smooth counterpoint to the texture of the fabrics.

Sleek curves and rounded forms imparted a feeling of sophistication and comfort while offering an interesting juxtaposition to the sharp, clean-lined proportions of each room. Subdued lighting not only highlighted the artwork but also drew the eye toward various areas within each space designed for a specific purpose: conversation, reading, eating, and so forth. In the living room, furniture was placed on an angle to enliven the rectangular space. Parquet floors were bleached and stained in a light tone, evoking a feeling of expansiveness and lending the space a minimalist tone.

The end result was a sophisticated and beautiful home that served as a gleaming showcase for the impressive collection of Picassos, Boteros, Nevelsons, Mirós, and other major artworks as well as an apartment that was a perfect space for entertaining guests.

Recently, these wonderful clients contacted me and requested that I return to their apartment to do an updated design. Their requirements remained the same: to focus the apartment's design on the art collection and to create a home conducive to a great deal of entertaining.

In the past twenty years, the interior design field has seen design approaches change based on strong economic influences on these trends. The 1970s was the era of minimalism—hard surfaces, focus on materials, and a lack of excessive ornamentation. In the 1980s, when the economy started to surge, interior design saw the reemergence of traditional decoration resplendent with a great deal of pattern, ornamentation, and detail. In the 1990s, the focus metamorphosed again to a more clean-lined and tailored

(continued on page 39)

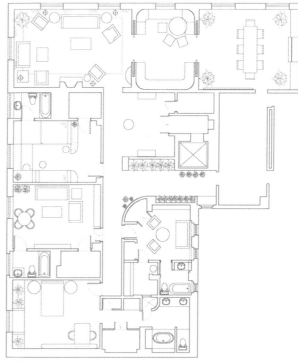

1998 design

DESIGN TIP

HIGHLIGHT ARTWORK AND DECORATIVE ACCESSORIES BY SELECTING NEUTRAL-TONED

COLORS THAT ALLOW THESE PIECES TO STAND OUT.

1978 design

Replacing the large contemporary painting with the Botero oil from the dining room further enhances the mood of the space. The gridded wood pattern created by raised panels (substituted for the quilted fabric walls) complements the stained parquet floors and the rounded shape of the Bauhaus–inspired table (one of my designs), the Henry Moore sculpture, and the subjects of the painting.

Textured wallpaper applied to resemble panels of parchment provides a subtle and elegant backdrop in the dining room. New chairs upholstered in an Art Deco fabric add a colorful note to the space. The pair of Botero sculptures remain in their original position, framing the doorway.

1978 design

1998 design

The living room still serves as a main entertaining space in the clients' home, but new upholstered pieces in a different arrangement give the room a softer, welcoming feeling. The custom carpet grounds the pieces and adds another level of comfort to the home. Window treatments, pillows, and fabric shades further promote the sense of comfort without detracting from the stunning artwork.

approach like the minimalist movement of the '70s, but with comfortable and softer details such as window treatments, fabric lampshades, decorative light fixtures, and pillows as influenced by the traditionalism of the '80s.

In the living room, a custom-designed carpet in a welcoming shade of sand grounds the new placement of the furniture. A stylized design in a slightly darker shade with black lines provides a visual accent and softens the geometric proportions of the space. Sophisticated, simple window treatments consist of side panels on a traverse rod, allowing the drapes to be drawn for added softness and privacy. A clean-lined valance tops each window. Tailored dressmaker details such as French seams and inverted pleats add a finished touch. Subtle striped fabrics, textural wallpaper applied as panels reminiscent of antique parchment, and deep wood tones make the room seem to glow in a welcoming manner. The pair of Mies van der Rohe chairs (reused from the previous design) combined with new eclectic accents, such as the pair of 1940s Regency—style floor lamps and the loose-cushion sofa, add a fresh look without overwhelming the art. The art has been rearranged and rotated into new locations, creating a completely different appearance. Deep claret serves as an accent color, further enhancing the overall sumptuous result.

1998 design

The light parquet floors throughout the home were stained to the darker, rich golden tone of the fine wood floors found in prewar New York City apartment buildings. The wall treatment in the foyer, originally a subtle quilted stripe, was replaced with a grid of raised wood panels. This visual background beautifully juxtaposes with the large rounded forms in the expansive oil painting by Fernando Botero and the Bauhaus–inspired chrome and granite table (which I designed) on which rests a sculpture by Henry Moore.

In the bedroom, the exquisite burled built-ins that comprise a desk, display ledge, and fireplace mantel remain, as does the upholstered banquette and platform bed. The only changes made are in the fabrics, carpeting, and window and wall treatments. To update the original bed design, all I did was add diminutive conical legs. The light rose-hued silk moiré fabric walls have been replaced with a beautiful golden glazed painted finish, complemented by the unstructured Roman shade that provides a sense of privacy, as well as a soft accent on the hard edge of the window frame. The custom-designed broadloom with a tone-on-tone pattern of interlocking circles recalls an arabesque pattern one might find in a beautiful Art Deco interior. A Chinese calligraphy-inspired fabric on the banquette cushions works nicely with the carpet on the platform. The graphic quilting on the bed cover fabricated in a windowpane stitch adds visual interest without overwhelming the

DESIGN TIP

REARRANGE EXISTING ARTWORK AND

FURNITURE BASED ON YOUR

INDIVIDUAL LIFESTYLE AND NEEDS.

THE END RESULT WILL AMAZE YOU.

1978 design

DESIGN TIP

UPDATE A PLATFORM BED BY ADDING

A SET OF NICELY FORMED LEGS.

RAISING THE MASS OF THE BED OFF THE

FLOOR IMPARTS AN AIRIER, MORE

UP-TO-DATE LOOK.

overall serenity of the design. A glass pendant fixture provides a decorative element to the room. This room serves as a private retreat as well as a contemplative place of repose.

As in the rest of the home, the dining room was "freshened up" by treating the walls and the floor in the same manner as the living room. A new collection of upholstered chairs, covered in a striking Art Deco fabric, encircles the dining table. The large Botero oil painting was moved to a prominent spot in the foyer, replaced by a pair of early twentieth-century posters, adding a festive note to the elegant dining room.

Designing a striking home to showcase an important and extensive art collection is a rare privilege. Getting the opportunity to do it twice is a distinct pleasure, especially when working with such interesting clients.

Placing the original bed on tapered conical legs gives the sleeping area more height. Warm golden tones and an unstructured Roman shade provide a feeling of warmth, comfort, and repose in the bedroom.

1998 design

CENTER STAGE

Designing for a client presents a specific set of challenges. These include dealing with budgets, different aesthetic perceptions, defined parameters, cherished objects, and other "givens" that must be worked with and around to create the perfect environment for the person. When designing a space for a showhouse, most of these restrictions do not exist; thus I have the freedom to design and create freely. The chance to try out something new, explore a new design treatment, and showcase a new fabric or piece of furniture is exciting and liberating. These design "experiments" allow me to grow as an interior designer and to display my talents and expertise for the general public. They can see firsthand the types of designs I create and the sense of my style aesthetic.

I designed my first showhouse room for the world-renowned Kips Bay Boys and Girls Club Decorator Showhouse in 1976. Kips Bay (as it is fondly known) is the premier showhouse in New York City and is eagerly anticipated each year as the major event in the New York interior design world.

My first foray into the showhouse world was a master bedroom in a large turn-of-the-century home on Fifth Avenue in New York City. I showcased many new design trends in this space: vertical blinds in lieu of more traditional window treatments, upholstered walls, sleek custom-designed furniture with European-influenced rounded corners and soft

(continued on page 47)

This master bedroom for the 1976 Kips Bay Showhouse featured many exciting new design elements: vertical blinds, an upholstered platform bed, Euro-influenced details such as the curved edges of the custom-designed furniture, and the unusual placement of the furniture focusing on the center of the space.

DESIGN TIP

TO CREATE A NEW AND EXCITING INTERIOR, TRY PLACING YOUR

FURNITURE IN THE CENTER OF YOUR ROOM. THIS TYPE OF FURNITURE

PLAN ALLOWS YOU TO MOVE FREELY ABOUT THE PERIMETER OF THE

SPACE, WHILE PROVIDING INTIMATE CONVERSATION AREAS.

This mood-evocative living room designed for the 1979 Kips Bay Showhouse found inspiration in the early twentieth-century French posters that serve as the prominent artwork in this space. The geometrically stenciled wood floor juxtaposes nicely with the sensuous furniture custom-upholstered in a vivid fuchsia fabric, a color with which I had always wanted to work but hadn't done so. A crystal Art Deco French chandelier, originally in a movie theater, crowns the room, while a 1930s satinwood grand piano anchors the space.

curves, and a highly unusual furniture placement scheme (the bed is in the middle of the room!). This showhouse space really introduced me to the general public as an interior designer and brought my work to the attention of the major home decorating and shelter magazines. I can honestly say that Kips Bay truly launched my interior design career.

Since my first showhouse room more than twenty years ago, I have created numerous spaces for various charity showhouses and fund-raising interior design events. This chapter highlights a small portion of these delightful rooms and serves as a window to a specific point in my interior design career. Each of these photographs provides a historical marker of where my design aesthetic was at that particular time and shows my growth as an interior designer. As a designer, I am constantly discovering new things and seeing everyday things in unusual and different ways. I meld these discoveries with my experience and education and incorporate these new elements into my designs. As I sit here reviewing these wonderful photographs, revisiting each space, and reminiscing fondly about these experiences, I am amazed to see that designs I created more than twenty years ago are still relevant and fresh today. Granted, I would change a few things as I have developed as an interior designer, but overall I am pleased to see that my work still embodies all the characteristics I want each of my designs to represent—beauty, functionality, comfort, and appropriateness.

Tranquillity and serenity are the keys to this grand salon I designed for the 1981 Kips Bay Showhouse. The white color scheme, bare wood floors, carefully selected accessories and artwork, and clean-lined furniture work together in this very strong architectural space to promote a feeling of comfort and peace.

Eclectic and opulent describe this wonderful space I designed for the 1985 Kips Bay Showhouse. This room represents a major turning point in my design direction from modern to a more traditional look, reflecting the "taste of the times." People knew me as a modern interior designer and this space showed the public that I could do traditionally inspired interiors as well. Fine antiques (such as the Biedermeier secretary by the window wall) and custom-designed pieces work beautifully in this large room. A grand-scale Aubusson needlepoint rug anchors the main sitting area directly in front of the soaring faux-limestone fireplace. The unusual curved staircase provides a sinuous counterpoint to the ziggurat-edged console placed next to it, both of which I designed.

DESIGN TIP

TO CREATE A MEMORABLE BEDROOM, BRING FOCUS TO THE MAIN

ELEMENT—THE BED—BY DRESSING IT UP TO BECOME THE CENTER OF

ATTENTION. YARDS OF FABRIC DRAPED ON A LARGE CANOPIED BED

PROVIDE A SUMPTUOUS AND SENSUAL REFUGE FROM THE WORLD.

This opulent French-inspired bedroom for the 1988 Kips Bay Showhouse sets a romantic and elegant mood, my personal interpretation of the late 1980s extravagance that was the norm in interior design. The large canopied bed swagged with many yards of cream-colored silk is reminiscent of a Balenciaga ballgown. Fine antiques, layers of window treatments, and separate his-and-hers baths make this bedroom suite an unforgettable showhouse room.

A tiny second-floor room was transformed in the 1991 Kips Bay Showhouse into a cozy space for an afternoon respite. The walls were decoratively painted in faux bois to look like curly maple. I selected Biedermeier antiques and accessories to further impart an elegant yet simple look. The complicated Neoclassic ceiling design complements the harlequin-patterned marble fireplace hearth. The broad black-and-white stripe of the upholstery fabric on the Biedermeier side chair provides a counterpoint to the serene quality of the other fabrics.

DESIGN TIP

MANY PEOPLE TEND TO IGNORE THE CEILING, BUT IT IS AN IMPORTANT PART OF ANY ROOM. BRING ATTENTION AND INTENSE INTEREST TO A

ROOM BY TREATING THE CEILING AS A BLANK CANVAS. THE ELABORATE NEOCLASSIC DESIGN PAINTED IN THE 1991 KIPS BAY SHOWHOUSE

PROVIDES THE MAJOR FOCAL POINT TO THE ROOM. THIS WORKS ESPECIALLY WELL IN A SPACE WHERE ARCHITECTURAL DETAIL IS LACKING,

OR IF THERE IS A MAJOR IMPERFECTION FROM WHICH YOU WANT TO DETRACT VIEWERS' ATTENTION.

This classically inspired library I designed for the 1994 Kips Bay Showhouse emphasizes the eclectic combination of fine antiques (primarily French Empire and Directoire), custom-designed furniture (such as the large celadon leather screen with the architecturally inspired nailhead design), and antique accessories. The oversized, custom-designed octagonal ottoman used as a coffee table adds a touch of warmth to the room.

Previous pages: This masculine and finely tailored library was my design for the 1998 Kips Bay Showhouse. My concept for the room was to use mostly twentieth-century furniture in an English eighteenth-century-style mahogany-paneled library to create a sense of tension and excitement. Strong clear colors, such as the mustard fabric on the sofa and the purple silk velvet on the armchair, give this room a rich and opulent appeal. Light-colored ceramic accessories in a plethora of shapes lend visual punch to the strong lines of the furniture.

DESIGN TIP

TO AVOID A STUDIED OR "TOO MUCH OF THE SAME THING" LOOK, TRY MIXING PIECES FROM DIFFERENT PERIODS AND STYLES TO ACHIEVE YOUR OWN PERSONAL DESIGN STATEMENT. ANTIQUES AND CONTEMPORARY PIECES CAN WORK TOGETHER IN A HARMONIOUS WAY IF THREE BASIC PRINCIPLES ARE APPLIED: USE SIMILAR SCALE (SIZE), SIMILAR SILHOUETTE (SHAPE), AND SIMILAR PROPORTION (VOLUME).

This bedroom I designed for the 1989 Southampton Showhouse combines fine Swedish antique furniture with simple linens and cotton voiles, a perfect combination for a summer resort community. Star-studded wallpaper provides a cheerful ground for the fine three-part antique English screen and the elaborate lis-à-la-polonaise bed. White muslin slipcovers and translucent fabrics provide the perfect look for a summer-inspired space.

This diminutive pool house was designed for the 1993 Southampton Showhouse as a personal retreat from the main house. Neutral fabrics, sinuously curved 1940s wrought-iron furniture, the stained wood floor left bare, and antique botanical prints infuse this pool house with the feeling of a summer living room. The scalloped edges of the ceiling trim are a reminder of summer pavilions prominent in the town of Southampton.

DESIGN TIP

IF YOUR HOME HAS WONDERFUL ARCHITECTURAL

DETAIL, BE CERTAIN TO BRING IT INTO THE

FOREFRONT BY SELECTING A COLOR SCHEME AND

FURNISHINGS THAT SHOWCASE THE DETAILS

RATHER THAN MASK THEM.

I designed this large living room for the 1994 Southampton Showhouse in a pastel and cream palette for a relaxed yet sophisticated atmosphere. Two comfortable back-to-back sofas are upholstered in cheerful linen floral with a French blue background that works wonderfully with the blue-and-white-striped unlined silk draperies. Touches of sunflower yellow add cheerful accent color to this room. The studied placement of the furniture creates various seating areas resulting in a comfortable, casual look without the appearance of clutter. The floor has been painted and stenciled in a trellis pattern of leaves, a subtle reminder of the gardens just outside the French doors that encircle the room.

In 1997 I designed this space for Mecox Gardens. Woven raffias (a return to the designs of the 1960s and '70s), strong-lined 1940s wrought iron, and natural wood and stone combine to create a sense of serenity and simplicity. A black-and-white still-life photograph in a natural gallery-style frame is the only artwork used on the walls. The checkerboard floor pattern in a colorway of cream and celadon gives the small space a sense of spaciousness. Beadboard paneling on the walls suggests a casual summerhouse feel. The overall effect was designed to showcase the late twentieth-century trend toward more modern interiors that emphasize texture and scale.

COASTAL RETREAT

Over the years I have worked on many different types of homes, from multiroom prewar duplexes on Park Avenue to brand new homes built in outlying areas surrounding the metropolitan region.

This house was built in 1880 in Connecticut on the shores of the Long Island Sound. This home, called Rockmere, is representative of the many large summer houses built at the end of the nineteenth century for city dwellers to use as their summer "cottages." They used these homes to escape from the heat of Boston and New York. I worked on the interior design of this home for very special clients who spend April to November here and the rest of the year in Palm Springs.

This approximately 7500-square-foot home had some architectural modifications, most notably a kitchen addition and library enlargement. The original architectural details and nuances of the house were kept intact and the interiors were designed to showcase them. The clients wanted their house to have a traditional feeling in keeping with the architecture and style of the home yet didn't want the house to be too formal; as their summer living quarters, the house needed to reflect their lifestyle and personalities.

A muted, serene palette of cream, ivory, and celadon predominates in most of the main public spaces of the home. These restrained colors give the house an airy, tranquil

(continued on page 62)

Located on the Connecticut shore of the Long Island Sound, this large summer "cottage" called *Rockmere* is a Victorian home built around 1880. I handled the interior design of the project, but the exterior kitchen addition and other architectural designs were created by John P. Franzen, AIA. The three-story shingle-style structure has many distinctive architectural features, including a porte cochere with a balcony located directly above it and two pairs of oval windows (known as oculuses) flanking the balcony and the porte cochere. A raised frieze of swags and garlands located directly at the edge of the hipped roof gives the home a classic look. Facing the Sound, the rear of the house has a fieldstone terrace leading to a pool area and a boat house (left). The entire enclave is perfectly suited for its waterside locale, a wonderful summertime retreat.

feel and allow the many architectural details to stand out. Crown moldings, dentil moldings, chair rails, dadoes, oval pass-throughs, raised panels, and other elements are painted a clean, refreshing white so they contrast with the wall color and upholstery used in each of the spaces.

Fine antiques share space beautifully with new contemporary pieces and custom upholstery. The floor in the living room is intentionally left bare to impart a summer house feeling to the room. A large trellis pattern of leaves painted onto the floor reflects the natural setting of the home and the gardens located just outside the windows. Touches of gold, silver, and crystal in selected furniture finishes, accessories, and lighting add shimmer and sparkle to the spaces, providing a nice counterpoint to the darker wood tones of the furniture and the floor. The fabrics selected for the upholstery and window treatments—cottons, linens, chenilles—are all appropriate for this summertime retreat. Heavy brocades and silks would not have been an appropriate choice: the end result would have been a fussy, heavy, airless interior that would be too staid and formal for this home and these clients.

The resulting design is exactly what the clients wanted and reflects them perfectly: a casual, sunny, spacious retreat that is elegant enough for entertaining, yet comfortable enough so that the family can live there every day and enjoy the many pleasures of this coastal home.

Filled with hydrangea and placed atop a painted Venetian chest, a pair of garden urns makes an elegant statement in the foyer of this home. The urns flank an oval pass-through that allows a glimpse of the living room just beyond.

The large living room is designed to provide spaces to converse, read, entertain, or just relax and enjoy the beautiful views of the Sound. The floor is stained a dark homey tone of brown with a graphic pattern of trellised leaves stenciled on top. Various styles and periods of furniture were selected for similar scale and shape, enabling them to blend harmoniously. Fabrics of varying shades of ivory also help unify the overall appearance of the room. The large-scale linen floral used for the draperies adds a punch of color and pattern to the room. Unstructured Roman shades fabricated from linen are hung directly above the windows and allow for light control. Accessories were selected for their beauty as well as to further promote the color scheme and overall feeling of relaxed elegance in the home. Built-in shelves contain an impressive collection of pottery and porcelain featuring a similar cream color and beautiful shapes.

DESIGN TIP

COLLECTIONS MAKE A GREATER IMPACT WHEN

THEY ARE DISPLAYED TOGETHER IN AN

ORGANIZED AND CAREFULLY EDITED MANNER.

Family photographs, comfortable upholstered pieces, and carefully selected accessories make this library a great spot to sit and read, play a friendly game of cards, or view the passing boats with the telescope located in the bank of windows. Neutral-toned colors give this room a sense of peace and calm. A subtle checked wall-to-wall carpet provides the inspiration for the checked pillows used to decorate the sofa. A large black wrought-iron chandelier, brass wall sconces, and ample table lamps provide sufficient illumination for any activity. The fireplace mantel is simply but elegantly adorned with a pair of weathered antique tole garden urns filled with hydrangea. A large painting by Milton Avery finishes the striking tableau.

DESIGN TIP

PAINT ARCHITECTURAL DETAILS WHITE

TO EMPHASIZE THEM.

A mahogany table (designed in our office) is flanked by upholstered French chairs in this elegant dining room. Unlined ivory silk drapes provide a soft accent at the windows and juxtapose well with the celadon green linen walls. A large antique Swedish crystal chandelier pairs nicely with the gilt mirror placed over the marble topped console table that serves as a handy sideboard; a pair of antique tole topiaries sit comfortably on top. The architectural details are painted a crisp white to stand out in this room without overpowering the objects within.

Eye-catching vertically striped wallpaper makes a distinctive accent in the billiards room. The striped multicolored carpet and the vertical lines of the rattan furniture playfully highlight this design element. Ship models, antique pull-toy replicas, colorful French posters from the early part of the last century, and of course, the billiards table, announce that this is a space designed for fun. A burnished red is used as an accent color in the shades of the light fixtures above the billiards table and in the check on the two armchair cushions.

DESIGN TIP

GRAPHIC ELEMENTS IN A ROOM CAN BE SUCCESSFULLY ENHANCED BY SUBTLY REPEATING

THEM; FOR EXAMPLE, IF YOU HAVE A VERTICALLY STRIPED WALLPAPER, CHOOSE FURNITURE

WITH STRONG VERTICAL LINES TO EMPHASIZE THIS DESIGN ELEMENT.

Originally an open-air porch, the sun porch provides a quiet spot to sit and read, relax, or enjoy a cup of morning coffee. Antique wicker furniture mixed with newer pieces provides an "outdoors" touch indoors. Potted plants in combination with garden elements and an abundance of light impart a "solarium" ambiance.

CHANDELIERS ARE NOT MEANT ONLY FOR THE DINING ROOM AND FOYER.

TRY USING ONE IN YOUR BEDROOM, LIVING ROOM, OR EVEN YOUR

BATHROOM TO CREATE A DISTINCTIVE AND HIGHLY PERSONAL LOOK.

Serene and tranquil are the key concepts behind the look I created for this master bedroom. A muted palette sets a tone of repose and relaxation. The crystal chandelier adds an elegant touch and works nicely with the mirrored commode used for a bedside table. Vertically striped glazed walls introduce subtle graphic interest without overpowering the space. The landscape painting strategically placed over the headboard provides a focal point within this room. The custom-designed coverlet, bed roll, and tailored bed skirt are in muted shades of ivory.

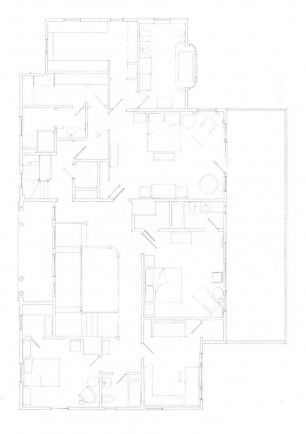

A bouquet of peonies and roses in soft pink, blush, and ivory is gathered in a simple crystal block vase. An antique Asian inlaid box, a round mother-of-pearl container, an antique alabaster vase, and a beautiful celadon ceramic lamp provide an assortment of interesting shapes and textures on the highly reflective top of the bedside mirrored commode.

Beadboard paneling used as a wainscotting adds graphic appeal in this new kitchen addition. A checkerboard border crafted of limestone tile defines the boundaries of the breakfast room. Six rush-seated chairs surround a round mahogany dining table. A simple but effective slipcover in a coordinating linen check covers the chair backs and echoes the grid established by the floor tiles. A large island occupies the center of the space and provides an additional spot for cooking. A brass chandelier, matchstick shades, and simple pendant fixtures impart an air of comfort and efficiency.

The foyer of this house is large enough to feature a seating area. A pair of French chairs upholstered in a tone-on-tone fabric features a complex pattern of interlocking curves, providing a nice geometric counterpoint to the ivory and sand stripe on the settee. An octagonal tea table placed directly in front of the settee serves as a spot to showcase a treasured objet d'art and a vase of peonies, fresh from the garden. The recessed panels of the wainscotting set a subtle graphic background to the ensemble. A pair of antique English botanical prints finishes the space.

The powder room located off the foyer on the first floor of the house boasts an oval window ("oculus") that serves as one of the more distinctive features of this house. A porcelain sink dropped into a sinuously curved marble countertop is supported by clear glass legs so it appears to be floating. A mural of the house's spectacular waterside location, painted by artist Diane Voyentzie, encircles the room. The perspective places the viewer on a cliff overlooking the scene.

A HAMPTONS RENAISSANCE

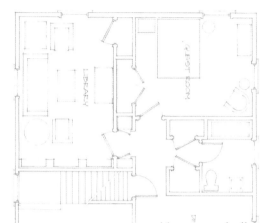

Designing the interiors for a client's vacation retreat or second home is a thrilling task. It allows me to really see how my clients live when they are not in their main home, what types of favorite pastimes and hobbies they pursue, and how they choose to relax and refresh themselves. It is definitely a fulfilling and exciting endeavor. But it can be difficult to create this special haven when your own country home is the one being designed.

A few years ago, my wife Lynn and I decided that we needed a country home to escape to during the hot, arduous days of summer and a special spot where we could retreat from the hustle and bustle of Manhattan. We wanted a home that was far enough away from New York City to feel as if we were truly getting away, but not too far that it would take an inordinate amount of time getting there and back. Additionally, our summer home would have to be large enough to accommodate our son, friends, and various family members who would come to visit. We like to entertain and we needed a house that would be elegant enough for company, but comfortable enough for the family to enjoy thoroughly when we were by ourselves.

After some reflection, we decided to purchase a modest two-story Cape Cod shingle-style home. Situated on the east end of Long Island, the house was built in 1954 and was structurally sound. The grounds, although not very well tended, were ample and the

(continued on page 80)

Before renovation

78

To complement the relaxed elegance of the home's interiors, the gardens and grounds were planted to resemble an English garden. The original driveway leading up to the original garage was designed to suggest a garden forecourt. Local wildflowers and well-tended stone-covered paths lead to the front door. The large architectural urn, pair of swags, and bracket add tremendous interest and detail to the front of our summer home. Garden paths and benches, and a swimming pool designed to resemble a reflecting pool work together to create a harmonious, natural environment.

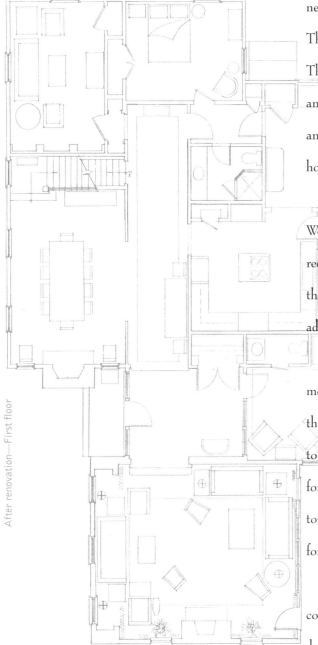

DESIGN TIP

SELECT FURNISHINGS THAT ARE APPROPRIATE

FOR YOUR FAMILY AND LIFESTYLE.

neighborhood was lovely, rural, and quiet (not to mention a short distance from the ocean). The original structure consisted of the main house, a connecting breezeway, and a garage. The house was in good condition, so our first step was to paint the entire first floor a clean and simple white, while we renovated the second floor where our bedroom, our son's room, and the laundry room were located. This initial simple renovation was done to make the house livable while we decided what we wanted to do for the final renovation.

Three years later we began the final renovation and the result turned out perfectly. We had the garage enlarged and made that the living room pavilion. The breezeway was redesigned to become our entrance foyer and the original living room was converted into the dining room. A study, larger kitchen, breakfast room, bathroom, and powder room were added onto the main house structure.

To achieve our chosen look of informal elegance, we used a traditional approach with a modern edge. Muted and subdued colors prevail throughout the interior of the home, with the exception of the vibrantly painted library. These subdued shades were specifically chosen to infuse an air of tranquillity and repose throughout our retreat. Shades of ivory and various forms of green—Lynn's and my favorite color—predominate. Fabrics in these same muted tones were selected for their textural and tactile quality. Patterns, where used, are straightforward and reflect the influences of the gardens and grounds surrounding the house.

The furniture is a collection of various styles and periods. Fine antiques mingle with comfortable upholstered pieces. Some of the occasional pieces are from the living room I designed for the 1994 Southampton Showhouse. Lynn and I bought this house at about the time I was doing the showhouse and I thought the furniture would be a perfect fit for our own summer home. The light whitewashed finish blends nicely with the warmer wood tones and lightens the overall effect of the interior design.

Our country home is the perfect reflection of my family's personality. It is a haven in this turbulent world and our favorite retreat.

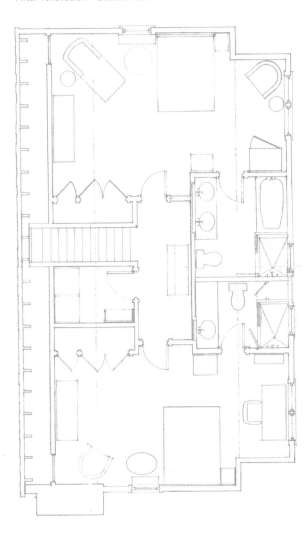

Wooded areas interspersed with paths covered in pine chips or flagstones provide leisurely spots for daily strolls. In addition, there are benches strategically placed along these paths that offer a contemplative spot to rest or reflect.

The overall design tone of our summer house is perfectly expressed in the foyer. Dark wood floors contrast with the cream-colored walls. A Neoclassic–inspired copper architectural frieze of urns and swagged garlands, originally used to decorate the exterior of a long-forgotten building, has been fitted to create a unique border. A pair of black wrought-iron plant stands serves as a subtle reminder of the gardens just outside the door and draws attention to the mood-evocative black-and-white photograph of a garden gate hung above the small settee. This wonderful piece, picked up for a few dollars, takes on a new life with a coat of white paint and a homey checked linen cushion.

A big antique table becomes the main focal point in the hallway. A large watercolor of a local scene provides graphic appeal. Further visual interest comes from a pair of black wrought-iron, nature-inspired sconces.

DESIGN TIP

TO CREATE A COHESIVE STYLE FOR YOUR SUMMER O

VACATION HOME, SELECT ONE COLOR PALETTE AND

REPEAT IT IN VARIOUS WAYS THROUGHOUT YOUR HOM

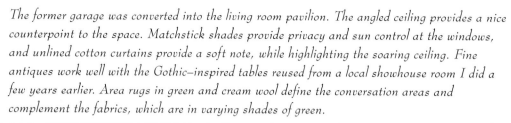

The former garage was converted into the living room pavilion. The angled ceiling provides a nice counterpoint to the space. Matchstick shades provide privacy and sun control at the windows, and unlined cotton curtains provide a soft note, while highlighting the soaring ceiling. Fine antiques work well with the Gothic–inspired tables reused from a local showhouse room I did a few years earlier. Area rugs in green and cream wool define the conversation areas and complement the fabrics, which are in varying shades of green.

DESIGN TIP

SELECT DECORATIVE ACCESSORIES

THAT REFLECT YOUR FAMILY'S

PERSONALITY AND INTERESTS.

The guest bedroom is a relaxing haven designed for visitors' comfort and pleasure. A queen-sized bedstead finished in faux bamboo is dressed in soothing antique linens and a piqué coverlet. Two antique side tables—one in bamboo the other with barley twist legs—provide ample space for illumination for bedtime reading or a cup of tea. A pair of antique bronze lamps complements the bedside tables' design. A soothing palette of cream and celadon predominates in the botanically inspired wallpaper selected for its reference to the beautiful gardens outside the windows. Simple tab café curtains in a white embroidered fabric afford privacy, as well as a soft note in the room.

A concrete vessel placed atop a vanity serves as the focal point of the powder room. A decorative paint finish in a strié pattern adds impact without overwhelming the prevailing air of serenity and tranquillity. A bamboo-framed mirror, painted to resemble tortoiseshell, adds a note of sophistication.

An antique mirror with a striking ebony frame makes a strong accent in the space. The bamboo and woven rattan chest of drawers is painted with a tortoiseshell finish, adding an exotic touch. A pair of star sconces adds ambient illumination.

Custom-designed cabinets painted in a pale blue-green endow the kitchen with a sophisticated country air. Open shelves above the countertops provide ample storage and display space for cherished objects. Stainless steel appliances in a brushed finish create glimmering accents. A porcelain tile floor laid in a contrasting pattern of green and beige squares lends graphic appeal. Bracket-style feet on all the cabinets give them the appearance of furniture rather than solid built-ins, enhancing the overall design.

DESIGN TIP

KEEP WINDOW TREATMENTS SIMPLE.

A botanical wallpaper based on a William Morris design sets the tone in the breakfast room. A soothing palette of green and ivory contrasts nicely with the dark tones of the round English mahogany dining table and chairs. The French wrought-iron chandelier works nicely with the wrought-iron framed mirror and flanking sconces. Simple wooden venetian blinds provide privacy as well as light control.

Sophisticated comfort prevails in the dining room. Pale yellow glazed walls serve as a calming backdrop for this elegant room. An antique ebony-framed circular mirror rests above a simple Georgian–style mantel with a tile hearth. Painted wooden shutters provide privacy as well as natural light control in the space. The warm tones of the wooden floor juxtapose nicely with the creamy finish of the dining table and vinyl and cotton upholstered chairs. An antique apothecary's chest topped with a piece of marble serves as a one-of-a-kind sideboard. A pair of quirky 1940s alabaster lamps provides additional ambient lighting.

A star-studded wallpaper in a blue colorway provides a soothing backdrop for my son's bedroom. A four-poster Anglo-Indian bed takes center stage. Crisp white Matelasse bed linens contrast nicely with the dark wood tones of the furniture. A pair of contemporary white ceramic lamps makes a strong accent and yields illumination for bedside reading.

The master bedroom is a cheerful retreat with its stylized gold and blue acanthus leaf
wallpaper. A beautifully carved late nineteenth-century French mahogany bed works nicely
with selected antiques and painted furniture pieces. Varying shades of gold fabrics accentuate
the wallpaper's palette. A cream-colored wool sisal wall-to-wall carpet anchors the various
pieces and provides comfort underfoot.

The overall white scheme of the guest bathroom offers a tranquil sanctuary for the visiting houseguest. An open-shelf under-cabinet furnishes plenty of linen storage. Antique black-and-white photographs by Lartigue of turn-of-the-century beach scenes provide visual interest. Polished brass hardware adds a touch of sparkle to the room.

The master bathroom was designed with comfort and ease in mind. The dual lavatory vanity topped with cream-colored marble provides ample room for my wife and I to get ready in the mornings. The recessed panels on the walls provide a subtle geometric pattern that highlights the graphic impact of the tumbled marble flooring. The large vanity affords sufficient storage, while a simple painted shelf keeps extra towels handy.

As in the rest of the home, the soothing palette of green and ivory predominates in the study. Comfortable upholstered pieces, finely selected antiques, and favorite objects and books infuse this room with our personality. A lyre-backed garden chair in an antique painted finish is reused from a showhouse space I designed in New York City a few years earlier. I fell in love with the chair's classical form and sleek silhouette, and bought it for a few hundred dollars. On a recent trip to France, I saw an almost identical chair for $40,000. I am so glad I decided to keep this charming piece for my own vacation home.

In contrast to the rest of the house, done in its soothing palette of celadon and cream, the library practically shouts in its cheerful tones of gold and red. These strong, warm colors make the room glow even on the cloudiest of days. The walls are covered in a natural grass cloth giving the room a British colonial feeling. The cheerful floral print on the sofa contrasts nicely with the multicolored striped carpet. A vintage rattan club chair, iron side table, and upholstered ottoman used as a coffee table infuse this space with a sense of comfort and ease, the primary prerequisites of a vacation home. Framed family photographs add a personal touch to the space.

AN ARTIST'S PALETTE

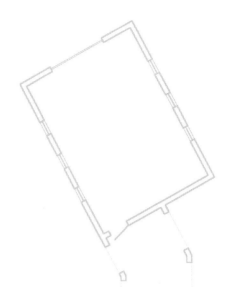

The traditional exterior of this Long Island home belies the interiors within. Verdant lawns, mature trees, potted plants, and shrubs add a natural touch to the home's white exterior. The unusual shape of the home as well as the hot pink pillows placed on the black awning-striped patio furniture provide a subtle design hint as to what is inside the home, just beyond the French doors.

I enjoy working with clients who have a vision, a direction for the design of their home. It gives me a framework to work within so that the final spaces are exactly what they desire.

This home on the east end of Long Island was designed for a couple who owns a prominent art gallery in the Hamptons. Their home is an essential haven from their hectic business, and also an important space for them to entertain guests, friends, and family. Their personal art collection is extremely significant to them, so the interior design needed to utilize their art as a major focus. However, these clients wanted lots of color in their home; they didn't want a monochromatic or neutral color scheme. Additionally, they wanted their home to reflect their eclectic taste.

The home is a welcoming mix of very different styles of furniture and features their wonderful art collection, including pieces by Milton Avery, Pete Turner, Horst, Matisse, Paul Resika, and Dan Rizzie. The rooms are designed with the art as focus, yet bright colors, vivid patterns, highly tactile textures, sinuous shapes, and various materials combine to create room designs that are fresh, current, whimsical, and highly unique. Custom-designed pieces, fine antiques, vintage objects, and contemporary furniture and accessories are blended in an individualistic and colorful style.

A piece of framed Chinese calligraphy rests against a Milton Avery pen-and-ink drawing. The shapely curves of the female figure in the drawing mimic the sensuous curves of the French iron console table. Flowers and leaves applied to the table base make a subtle reference to the country location of this spectacular home.

A close-up of the same grouping shows the masterful juxtaposition of angular furniture pieces with curved ones placed atop the circular area rug. The entire room is a subtle study of geometric shapes and their playful positioning within the home. Adjacent to the sitting room, the dining room is just visible to the rear. Unadorned windows allow plenty of natural sunlight to fill the home.

A circular area rug with a stylized pattern of leaves and vines anchors an informal conversational grouping in the center of the sitting room. An antique French daybed upholstered in black ottoman cloth contrasts nicely with two antique country chairs finished in white and upholstered in a casual yet sophisticated check of black-and-white cotton. Two green silk throw pillows with Turkish corners give a jolt of color to the black-and-white scheme. The conversation group appears to be a welcoming island situated on the black enameled floor.

A natural brick floor, painted white and left bare, provides a nice geometric background for the dining room. A long, custom-designed rectangular table with a stylized iron base is surrounded by upholstered French chairs, which are finished in antique white paint and covered with a green silk. A beautiful hand-painted casement fabric is used for the tailored window treatments. A playful interlocking design of curves and squiggles adds a whimsical touch to the neutral-toned window treatments.

Family photographs, potted plants, vases of cut flowers, and favorite books infuse each room throughout the home with a sense of the family. I think it's very important to establish the personality of the homeowners in every room. This gives the house its individual character and its sense of being. It lets everyone who visits discover who lives there and what they are all about.

Working on this project allowed me to create a spectacular residence that is a one-of-a-kind home. What a pleasure to have the opportunity to design spaces with other creative people.

I designed the library as a cozy retreat with an exotic flair. Built-in bookcases blend beautifully with the upholstered walls. A plump two-cushion sofa covered in a sand chenille complements the wall color and the cream tone of the wall-to-wall wool carpet. A beige-and-mauve striped fabric is used on a pair of club chairs I designed to coordinate with the sofa; their nice tailored details make them a bit more special. Decorative accessories and objets d'art from my clients' travels and personal collection finish the space. A Roman shade crafted from fabric with a repeating print of animals in a vertical stripe highlights the upholstery on the club chairs and reinforces the exotic theme.

The exotic pattern of the enameling on this glass table lamp adds graphic interest to this library tableau. The round shape of the porcelain bowl mimics the moss sphere placed simply on a terra-cotta saucer. A single stalk of ornamental kale makes a striking and highly unusual floral arrangement. The vivid colors of the photograph of a young African girl, by Pete Turner, provide a delightful and poignant accent.

Black-and-white woven café chairs provide comfortable seating in the light-filled breakfast room. The subtly patterned wallpaper adds visual interest to the room without overwhelming the ambiance of serenity and tranquillity. Café curtains are fabricated from an ivory casement with a woven pattern of leaves. The harlequin-patterned valance has a zigzagged hem to highlight the diamond shapes of the fabric. A vintage French Directoire chandelier in the shape of a lyre (which I found in Paris) hangs above the marble-topped pedestal table with a black wrought-iron base.

The hallway features a large contemporary painting by Dan Rizzie positioned directly above a stylized metal bench. On the floor, the painted diamond pattern in contrasting tones of gold, ivory, and cream guides the viewer to the artwork.

DESIGN TIP

DISPLAY YOUR FAVORITE PIECES OF

ARTWORK PROMINENTLY AND SELECT

FURNISHINGS THAT ENHANCE BUT

DON'T OVERWHELM THEM.

A classically inspired 1940s console provides ample display space in this corner of the living room. The exaggerated sweep of the curved legs lends a contemporary touch to the more traditional reeded decorations on the console legs and the nearby painted French chair. A potted orchid, piles of art books, and a footed alabaster bowl filled with a trio of lemons forms a memorable vignette. The oil painting by Paul Resika hanging over the console directs the eye toward this corner of the room, with its deep, vivid colors and strong graphic shapes. On the adjacent wall, the black-and-white drawing by Esteban Vicente subtly continues the strong geometry of the room.

An eclectic mix of furniture provides comfort and a finely tuned sense of individual style in the living room. A big wool sisal area rug in a neutral sand tone provides a soothing backdrop for the main conversation area. A large abstract painting by contemporary artist Connie Fox predominates in the room. A beautiful Venetian mirror above the fireplace is flanked by a pair of mirrored candle sconces, designed by Herve van der Straeten, to give the room a glimmering accent. Simple cotton batiste curtains hung on rings and suspended from black wrought-iron rods provide natural light control while softening the sharp angles of the room.

A simple decorative vignette on top of an unusual side table of spread-winged eagles creates a striking living-room tableau. A natural bouquet of vividly colored zinnias adds a shot of color. A curved blue bowl, an alabaster bottle, an alabaster box, and an unusual contemporary silver-leafed table lamp continue the spherical shapes that predominate in the display. A black-and-white drawing by Esteban Vicente adds additional graphic appeal.

The upstairs gallery in this artistic home provides enough space for a conversational grouping, as well as sufficient wall and floor space to display prized artwork. The shiny black enamel paint of the bare floors contrasts strongly with the colorful art. A large still life by Dan Rizzie adds color to the gallery.

DESIGN TIP

COLOR CAN PROVIDE TREMENDOUS

VISUAL INTEREST IN YOUR HOME. DON'T

BE AFRAID TO TRY A NEW COLOR THAT

YOU'VE ALWAYS LOVED. BUT IF YOU'RE

HESITANT TO PAINT AN ENTIRE ROOM

ONE OF YOUR FAVORITE COLORS,

EXPERIMENT WITH A FEW PILLOWS OR

DECORATIVE ACCESSORIES IN THAT

COLOR TO TRY IT OUT.

DESIGN TIP

WHEN YOU SELECT FURNITURE PIECES IN SIMILAR

SHAPES AND FORMS YOU CREATE A "DESIGN

RHYTHM" THAT HAS A STRONG VISUAL IMPACT.

CONVERSELY, JUXTAPOSING DIFFERENT SHAPES AND

FORMS PREVENTS YOUR ROOMS FROM LOOKING TOO

SIMILAR AND CREATES A ONE-OF-A-KIND INTERIOR IN

YOUR HOUSE WITH INTERESTING VISUAL TENSION.

With its soaring ceiling and shocking pink walls, this guest bedroom exudes a sense of 1930s Hollywood glamour and drama. The French upholstered headboard with its acanthus leaf carving and patterned button tufts provides a geometric counterpoint to the overall sense of softness and romanticism. Voluptuous curtains in a pristine white soften the angles of the room and provide light control and privacy at the Palladian windows. A thick shag-style white area rug softens the black painted floor and furnishes an additional note of comfort in this bedroom. A pair of crystal table lamps, the mirrored bedside console, and the mirrored and crystal tea table in front of the sofa add sparkle and glimmer to this sensuous room.

DESIGN TIP

MIRRORS AREN'T JUST FOR THE WALL. TODAY YOU CAN

USE MIRRORED FURNITURE (VINTAGE, NEW, OR

ANTIQUE) TO ADD SHIMMERING ACCENTS TO ANY ROOM.

The large black-and-white photograph by Lorraine Shemesh gives a focal point to the seating area in the guest bedroom. A stylized Ionic column floor lamp, originally from the Eden Roc Hotel in Miami Beach, adds a whimsical note while repeating the playful interaction of forms found throughout the home. Upholstered in a very deep shade of bright pink linen, a whimsical Venetian side chair features exaggerated curves and lines that make it seem to dance. When a room contains striking and colorful furniture pieces, the accessories should enhance and not overwhelm the other design elements. I placed a serene bouquet of blush-colored roses in the center of the mirrored tea table. The soft tones of the flowers contrast with the striking hues of the walls, and the romantic touch of fresh roses further enhances the ambiance of this guest bedroom.

The etched and mirrored bedside console lends a memorable note to this bedroom. I purposefully composed a subdued vignette for the top of it so as not to detract from the beauty of the furniture piece. A large contemporary silver-leafed vase holds a bunch of lilies and mums.

DESIGN TIP

TO MAKE DIFFERENT VINTAGES AND STYLES OF FURNITURE WORK TOGETHER, SELECT FABRIC IN COLORS AND PATTERNS THAT COMPLEMENT AND UNIFY THE LOOK OF THE PIECES. ALSO, CHOOSE FINISHES THAT VISUALLY MATCH THE FURNITURE INSTEAD OF HIDING THE INDIVIDUAL BEAUTY OF EACH PIECE SELECTED.

A black-and-white drawing by Henri Matisse is prominently displayed in the seating area of the master bedroom. The silver-leafed frame and soothing color combinations work well with the tranquil palette used throughout the master bedroom. A contemporary floor lamp finished in silver leaf complements the picture frame as well as the mirror and crystal vintage tea table. Brush fringe placed along the bottom of the lampshade adds a whimsical touch to the room.

Center stage in this master bedroom goes to the draped four-poster iron bed. A neutral palette of ivory, cream, and silver with strong accents of black and gold adds interest and contrast. Wall-to-wall geometric-patterned carpet in creamy tone-on-tone shades provides comfort underfoot, while unifying the eclectic collection of furniture.

Black-and-white toile sets a classical theme in the master bathroom. A decoupaged antique cabinet serves as a perfect storage piece for linens while providing ample display space on top. Bathroom essentials in combination with decorative accessories and a wonderful old apothecary flask create a vignette that is homey while at the same time sophisticated. An antique landscape print leaning against the wall provides visual interest, while a small gilt-frame silhouette lends a decorative touch to the tabletop display.

A mirrored 1920s French dressing table makes a sparkling accent in the master bedroom. Assorted sterling silver-topped flasks, bottles, jars, and containers enhance the silvery gleam of the table, while their rounded shapes echo the circular form of the mirror. A pair of unusual Art Deco obelisk-shaped dresser lamps illuminate the tabletop display. A duet of crystal bud vases adds height to the tableau and balances out the bouquet of roses at the opposite side of the dressing table. A photograph of a favorite vacation spot serves as a nostalgic remembrance.

THE FINISHING TOUCH

Though I've been an interior designer for years, it never ceases to amaze me how a room doesn't come to life until the accessories and artwork are added. Once these vignettes and tabletop displays are established in a space, the room acquires its own unique personality and that of the people who inhabit it.

Color selection; wall, window, and floor treatments; furniture placement; fabric usage; architectural details; and other major design elements are vital to the foundation of good interior design, but the accessories and artwork are what add the finishing touch to make a space entirely its own.

The same basic principles that are applied to the major aspects of interior design relate to tabletop vignettes: scale and proportion, style, silhouette (shape), material (what something is made of), color, and usage (appropriateness). When these basic principles are utilized to finish a room, the results are the same as when they are applied to the major aspects of the interior's design: good, solid design with a unique and personal character.

I also remind myself how important it is for my clients and anyone who is designing their home to use the belongings they love and delight in to finish their spaces. I don't create interiors for my clients with my possessions or objects; I use things they love and enjoy making a part of their daily lives. By using favorite belongings in your personal spaces, your home acquires your personality and allows guests and visitors to glimpse your family's personal side. It lets people know what you like to do in your spare time, what hobbies and pastimes you pursue, and what things you and your family enjoy collecting and displaying.

Rooms that lack personality offer no insights into the people who live in and use them every day. Family photographs, special mementos, cherished collections, travel souvenirs, beloved heirlooms, and artwork that "means something" all contribute to making our homes uniquely our own—personal havens from the hustle and bustle of the daily grind we all must face.

Every new project affords me great design challenges and opportunities to grow as an interior designer. Using my clients' private treasures and special *objets d'art* gives me the chance to learn about them as people and to enjoy this wonderful aspect of my profession.

DINING AND TEA TABLES

Above: In this sitting room, designed for the Abigail Adams Showhouse in New York City, an antique mahogany English tea table is the focal point of the conversational grouping of furniture. The beautiful Spode tea service is decorated with a stylized acanthus leaf pattern that mimics the sinuous lines of the vines embellishing the six-panel screen behind the settee. A single-footed brass candlestick adds a tall counterpoint to the relatively low height of the other objects.

Below: A close-up detail of the tea table display emphasizes the graphic quality of the porcelain tea service and how it juxtaposes beautifully with the graphic vertical stripe of the linen slipcovers.

Above and Right: A skirted circular dining table is located in another corner of the sitting room I designed for the Abigail Adams Showhouse. Pieces from the Spode tea service combine with a wonderfully detailed creamware teapot, footed creamware compote to display pastries, and a footed antique pressed-glass compote filled with green apples. With its veined texture and different height, an alabaster candlestick provides a striking note while accentuating the vertical stripes of the slipcover fabric, as well as the fluting on the nearby column supporting the Boston fern. My favorite little garden chair (which I picked up for a few hundred dollars and is now comfortably ensconced in my study on Long Island) is pulled up to the table. The vertical lines of the lyre splat mimic the verticality of other elements in the room.

I used this octagonal antique tea table in a client's study in New Jersey instead of the usual coffee table for a number of reasons. The height of the tea table provides a convenient spot to rest a book or a cup of tea and it makes a nice spot to display a trio of porcelain French boxes and a hand-blown Venetian glass vase. The spherical shape of these objets d'art contrast nicely with the angular shape of the table, while complementing the silhouette of the round pillow on the sofa and the antique Victorian tufted footstool located nearby.

Below: This Art Deco–inspired dining room uses period candlesticks and beautifully designed china and flatware to reinforce the theme. A large period oil painting of two women sharing a meal enhances the overall feeling created in this space.

Above: I chose a magnificent gilded tea table for this elegant living room. The two objects used to decorate the top of the table emphasize the overall ambiance of sophistication and formality established by the pair of antique chairs placed directly across from the gilded framed diminutive settee. When creating sophisticated vignettes for elegant rooms such as this one, be certain to select pieces that are important enough to stand on their own. Here, the shallow shape of the fine white porcelain bowl contrasts beautifully with the vertical silhouette of the antique decorative compote. Keeping the tabletop vignette simple serves to enhance the beauty of the elaborately carved base of the tea table and the fine lines of the other furniture pieces.

DESKS

Below: The clean lines and imposing scale of this 1930s French desk is enhanced by the placement of carefully selected objects. A pair of contemporary bronze lamps flank either end of the desktop, while the center portion is filled with leather desktop accessories, a spherical crystal vase sporting brightly colored blooms, a sterling silver inkwell, and a round standing mirror in a chrome frame. The contrasting shapes and varying heights of the resulting tableau effectively combine to excite the viewer's eye.

Above: This antique French Empire desk is a breathtaking example of the influence of classical design on interiors. The symmetrical placement of the fine antique objets d'art in combination with the Louis XV sconces and pair of landscape oil paintings augments the style of this room and the strong design of the antique desk.

Above: The back view of this desktop tableau shows how the playful juxtaposition of shapes is further enhanced by the mono-chromatic pottery placed around the room on top of the bookcases. Notice how the lamp bases mimic the shapes of these vessels in a subtle and sophisticated manner.

Below: A close-up view of this desktop demonstrates how the rounded shapes of the vase, flowers, inkwell, and mirror create a strong design statement by being clustered together on this expansive piece of furniture.

Above: This Neoclassical–style desk is topped with a collection of obelisks crafted out of various materials. The differing heights of these architectural souvenirs contrast nicely with the rectangular shape of the antique box and framed family photographs. The large bronze medallion, vintage 1930s, increases the visual impact of this vignette. On a nearby windowsill, the painted wooden Buddha adds a further exotic note.

Below: The collection of obelisks is graphically shown in this detail photograph of the desktop (above). Note how the bronze griffin further imparts a classical tone to the tabletop display.

A mirrored Art Deco desk serves double duty as a desk cum side table in this clean-lined interior. Careful positioning of decorative and desk accessories strengthens the details of the mirrored table.

MIRRORS AND ART

Below: A round table is placed next to a club chair and ottoman in this library I designed for the 1998 Kips Bay Showhouse. A vase of strikingly hued flowers and a shagreen box are the only adornments on the tabletop, resulting in a simple, memorable vignette. A lacquered Art Deco screen filled with images of machine-age shapes reiterates the circular form of the table and the piece of sculpture on the mantel placed directly in front of a mirror.

Above: Flanking an antique coffer with a pair of fifteenth-century wood and gesso Italian statues yielded this elegant and beautiful display. The wonderful patina of these pieces enhances the feeling of classical antiquity I sought to create in this home. The gilded marble-topped Rococo console is an elegant piece by itself, but when paired with an elaborate mirror, French Louis XV sconces, and fine decorative objects symmetrically placed on top, the result is a classic and elegant tableau.

Below: This marble-topped demi-lune console supports a massive painted and gilded urn. The architectural shape of the important object on the table is reflected in the mirror-framed antique architectural drawings hung directly above.

Above: A segmented cylindrical vase topped with a pyramid of lemons is placed next to a mirror in this impressive mantel-top display. Note that the mirror is leaned against the wall instead of being hung. The result is refreshing and spontaneous.

DESIGN TIP

WHEN DISPLAYING AN IMPORTANT DECORATIVE OBJECT OR PIECE OF ART, GIVE IT MORE IMPORTANCE WITHIN A SPECIFIC ROOM BY SHOWCASING IT ALONE RATHER THAN WITH A GROUP OF OTHER OBJECTS.

Below: An oval wire-framed mirror lends a sculptural look to this living room. I placed a potted ivy to one side of the mirror to give the mantel an asymmetrical look that corresponds with the asymmetrical placement of architectural and collected objects on the built-in shelves flanking the fireplace. The result is fresh and very current.

Above: Placed prominently above the sofa, the large oil painting of a pair of leopards imparts an exotic flavor to this study. The four-part pierced wooden screen, the collection of Chinese porcelains on top of the armoire, and other unusual accessories further enhance this feeling.

Below: A simple gilded framed mirror enhances the classically inspired tableau placed on top of this contemporary mantel. An elaborate antique Biedermeier clock fitted with ormolu is flanked by a pair of marble-base urns and porcelain plates. The resulting symmetrical vignette emphasizes the clean-lined symmetry of the room reflected in the mirror.

DESIGN TIP

TO CREATE A DISPLAY WITH A

CLASSICAL OR MORE FORMAL FEELING,

PLACE OBJECTS IN A SYMMETRICAL

PATTERN ON TABLETOPS, SHELVES, OR

MANTELS. PAIRS OF OBJECTS WORK

EXTREMELY WELL FOR THIS

PARTICULAR TYPE OF DESIGN.

END TABLES

Below: Beautiful tables require accessories that will enhance and not detract from their special status. The unusual arrangement of this trio of woven rattan tables is highlighted by the trio of decorative spheres placed on top. An ivy topiary and a black-and-white photograph further imbue this serene setting with a dash of visual interest.

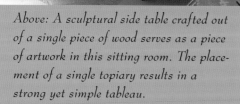

Above: A sculptural side table crafted out of a single piece of wood serves as a piece of artwork in this sitting room. The placement of a single topiary results in a strong yet simple tableau.

Above: This tile-topped end table in a colorway of blue, white, and yellow holds a collection of silver boxes in varying shapes. These diverse shapes playfully emphasize the natural grid created by the tiles. A blue-and-white porcelain dish reiterates the hand-painted qualities of the tile and the color scheme. A simple table lamp and a vase of roses finish off this charming tableau.

Below: This unusual end table is placed next to a sofa in a study. A trio of wooden boxes and an important family photograph (framed in sterling silver), create an elegant vignette.

Left: A Gothic–inspired side table is topped with a simple display composed of an antique floral porcelain pitcher and a classically inspired urn-shaped lamp.

DESIGN TIP

WHEN DISPLAYING PHOTOGRAPHS, SELECT FRAMES MADE OF SIMILAR MATERIAL OR CREATED IN A SIMILAR STYLE. THE RESULT IS A MORE UNIFIED AND COHESIVE LOOK THAT DOESN'T DETRACT FROM THE PHOTOGRAPHS.

A metal table with a faux marble top provides a wonderful stage for a gilded urn lamp based on an architectural detail, a trio of cherished family photographs in sterling silver frames, and a simple white porcelain bowl.

Above: The same tabletop as that at the top left acquires a completely different feeling with a quartet of inexpensive small glass vases, each containing a single blossom. An arched photo frame echoes the arches of the table's base and the curves of the urn lamp.

Below: An inlaid star pattern embellishes the top of this end table. I kept the accessories to a minimum so the beautiful table would take center stage. I even chose a floor lamp instead of a table lamp so that more of the tabletop would show.

Right: A vase of flowers, a sculptural glass table lamp, a pair of framed photographs, and a simple white porcelain bowl result in a contemporary vignette highlighting the black-and-white drawings hung directly above the tabletop. The table is from a collection that I designed in the mid-1990s.

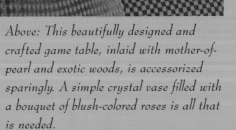

Above: This beautifully designed and crafted game table, inlaid with mother-of-pearl and exotic woods, is accessorized sparingly. A simple crystal vase filled with a bouquet of blush-colored roses is all that is needed.

Above: A collection of mercury glass vases emphasizes the reflective quality of this two-tiered mirrored end table.

Left: The sculptural qualities of the display can be appreciated in this close-up view of the tabletop. The rounded forms of the vases, vessel, and bowl reinforce the circular shape of the table in a subtle yet distinct manner.

Left and Above: Clustering similar objects in groupings of three or more gives them greater impact. Here a pair of vases, a long-necked vessel, and a black bowl gain prominence through the repetition of similar shapes and forms.

DESIGN TIP

IF YOU HAVE A SPECIAL OR SIGNIFICANT TABLE, DON'T OBSCURE IT BY ARRANGING TOO MANY THINGS ON TOP. IF YOU MUST USE THE TABLE FOR DISPLAY, KEEP IT SIMPLE SO AS NOT TO DETRACT FROM THE FURNITURE PIECE ITSELF.

Above: A quartet of inlaid boxes in combination with the Chinese porcelain lamp enhance the ambiance of this colorful study. The red-and-black lacquered end table works in conjunction with the accessories placed on its top to reinforce this design element.

CREATIVE TABLETOP DISPLAYS: HOW-TOS

Below: The sinuous curves of this coffee table (from the 1998 Kips Bay Showhouse) are accented by the rounded form of the lacquered Chinese box and the antique bronze sculpture placed on top. To craft the unusual moss centerpiece, I simply planted a natural wood tray with sheet moss. The resulting rounded forms are exactly what I wanted to use in this clean-lined, masculine library.

Above: A bamboo nightstand is topped with a barley-twist lamp and a collection of favorite seashells we picked up along the beach near our summer home. The resulting vignette is a beautiful, simple design.

Left: The close-up photograph of the tabletop (top left) highlights the sculptural quality of the seashells. The textural look of the table's wood grain and the natural beauty of the bamboo add to the simple beauty of this tableau.

DESIGN TIP

CLUSTER SIMILAR OBJECTS TO CREATE

A VIGNETTE WITH MORE IMPACT.

Below: This bedside table provides ample space to rest a book, a cup of tea, or a pair of reading glasses. It also serves as a stage to showcase a collection of American pottery. The pastel colors and floral design on the pottery add a soft decorative accent to this tableau.

Below: A French iron side table provides ample space when used as a nightstand. A black wire urn lamp reinforces the round shape of the vintage Bakelite alarm clock. The clear glass vase (a souvenir from a florist's gift arrangement) is filled with dried hydrangea from the garden.

Above: The sunlight casts shadows of the wire lamp, creating patterns on the metal surface of the table.

Right: A detail of the vignette (top right) beautifully illustrates the successful pairing of the pottery's glaze and the rich green color of the table.

DESIGN TIP

SELECT ACCESSORIES OF SIMILAR

SHAPES, SILHOUETTES, AND FORMS.

CLUSTERING THESE ITEMS CREATES

A SUBTLE DESIGN RHYTHM THAT

HELPS TO REINFORCE THE LOOK YOU

WISH TO ACHIEVE IN YOUR HOME.

Below: A quintet of pressed-glass cake pedestals creates a surprising and effective method of raising the topiaries off this tabletop to avoid a cluttered and crowded look. The plants seem to float above the table, allowing the striking wood grain to dominate. An old sundial face (picked up at a tag sale for a dollar) adds a strong graphic element to this tableau.

Below: A tablescape detail illustrates the different patterns of each pedestal and how the sunlight streaming in the nearby window makes the glass sparkle, creating interesting shadows and forms on the tabletop.

Above: In today's home, spaces have to serve many functions, and so too should the furniture. Instead of using the customary coffee table, I designed a wonderful uphol-stered ottoman for this library. Not only does it serve as a place to display favorite books and accessories, it can also be used as a footstool, a chair, or a serving spot.

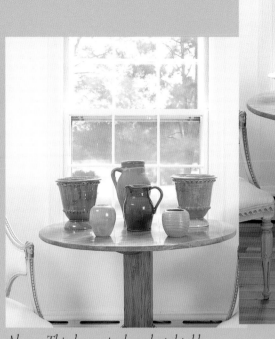

Left: The same table takes on a completely different appearance with a change of accessories. The more relaxed and comfortable look is achieved by placing a bouquet of sunflowers in an inexpensive galvanized flower bucket (available at any gardening center) and finishing off the tableau with a pile of books, a rectangular white porcelain dish (an airline dish purchased from a factory outlet store), and an antique creamware bowl filled with a trio of wooden bocce balls (rescued from the attic).

Above: This large single-pedestal table holds a collection of colorful pottery. The shapes and symmetrical placement of the pottery reinforce the lines and style of the classically inspired table.

DESIGN TIP

ALTER THE LOOK OF A ROOM SIMPLY BY

CHANGING THE TABLETOP VIGNETTES. TRY TO

ALTER THE HEIGHTS OF OBJECTS ON DISPLAY.

THINGS OF THE SAME HEIGHT APPEAR FLAT TO

THE EYE, WHILE VARIOUS-SIZED OBJECTS

EXCITE AND MAKE THE EYE TRAVEL.

Above: An inexpensive iron side table is topped with a turned wooden-base lamp, pieces of favorite pottery, and a small topiary. The position of the pottery and the topiary (slightly taller than the pottery) draws the eye upward toward the pleated checked lampshade.

Above: Common objects found around the home take on a new perspective when used as decorative objects on this same tabletop. A wire basket filled with green and red apples adds a dash of color. A domino game in progress adds a nice decorative touch, as well as an enjoyable pursuit while sitting with a guest.

Above: The tabletop takes on a completely different appearance when the basket of apples and dominoes are replaced with a vintage lawn bowling set. The well-worn patina of the pins and ball works comfortably with the table's worn finish.